THE POWER
— OF —
THE PRIDE

Best wishes
Ian Thomas
2014

THE POWER
OF
THE PRIDE

IAN THOMAS

As far as possible photographs of the actual event have been used.
Where they were not available,
photographs that closely illustrate the text were used.

Text and photographs © World-wide Ian Thomas.

All photographs were taken by Ian Thomas
except pages 27 & 29 by Colin Bell of Wilderness Safaris.

Published by Ian Thomas
P.O. Box 651521, Benmore, 2010 Republic of South Africa.
Tel: (+27 11) 883-2088 Fax: (+27 11) 883-2600 e-mail: info@ianthomas.net
www.ianthomas.net
ISBN. No. 978-0-620-17025-3

First published 1992

Desktop publishing by Anne Centner

Design by Johan Hoekstra

Edited by Denis Smith

Colour reproduction by Repro Solutions

Printed by Tien Wah Press (Pte) Ltd.

CONTENTS

ACKNOWLEDGEMENTS

Business and wildlife have been the two subjects most often discussed around the dinner table and campfire by my family and for that I have to thank my parents, Arthur and Helen, and my three brothers, Grant, Peter and Neil.

A special thank you to my wife, Moira, and our two children, Clyde and Lara.

Thanks are also due to Anne Centner, my desktop publisher; Johan Hoekstra, who designed this book; and Prue Johnson, who typed it.

Denis Smith deserves a medal for deciphering my handwriting.

I could fill another volume with the names of the many fine friends, businessmen and women who have given me the encouragement and inspiration I needed to complete this book. They will know who they are and I hope they will accept my humble and sincere gratitude.

Ian Thomas

DEDICATION

This book is dedicated to "Big Black",
the most awesome lion I have ever encountered.

To Winnis Mathebula, who loved tracking lions;
the thicker the bush, the deeper the donga, the more he liked it.

To Phineas Mhlongo, a superb tracker
of an extremely dangerous lion.

AUTHOR'S NOTE

THE STUDY OF LIONS in the wild has involved me in far more than the gathering of biological data. Discussions with businessmen and women while viewing lions has made me aware of the social interaction, hunting techniques and defence strategies among individual lions with vastly different personalities, strengths and weaknesses.

Hearing comments such as "I wish my team communicated like that lion pride" planted in my mind the idea of a business presentation which would point out the analogies between business teams and lion prides. This presentation has been hugely successful in southern Africa, Europe and the United States.

Many friends in business and wildlife management provided input which persuaded me to turn the successful presentation into this book – The Power of the Pride.

It has never been my intention to make comparisons between lionesses and women in business nor between lions and men in business. Neither have I tried to draw direct comparisons between lion prides and business teams, preferring simply to make clear that the one can learn a lot from observing the other and using what is applicable to them.

My love affair with wildlife has been incredibly rewarding. To me there is nothing more beautiful than the grace and power of a big cat – nothing which represents the thunder of Africa more than the full-blooded roar of a lion.

THE PRIDE IS BORN

THE PRIDE STRUCTURE developed on the great grassy savannahs of Africa, a veld rumbling with wild animals, where even today roam vast herds of antelope and zebra. Lions evolved alongside the herds and the interaction between hunter, hunted and competitor forged lions into teams of superbly effective hunters and fighters.

Most felines are loners. However, a single lioness, no matter how skilled or desperately hungry, would often be outmanoeuvred and overwhelmed by her robust and alert prey.

The answer lay in ambush. A simple technique and completely effective.

The lioness waits in hiding. Her pride-mates drive the prey into the trap.

A simple technique – but so effective that lions excelled and the pride was born.

Lion prides consist of a flat social structure in which lions and lionesses, powerful individuals in their own right, benefit from belonging to a group of equally powerful members all motivated by the same clear-cut goals.

This immensely efficient formation puts the lion pride in a win-win situation where the success of each individual is the team's success – and the success of the team is the success of each individual.

A pride of lions is an example of teamwork for maximum effect.

This book explains how it works for them and how it can work for you.

HUNTING

LIONESSES DO MOST of the hunting.
Older females bring their superior strength,
maturity and experience to the hunt – the
younger animals provide the speed, agility
and energy.

Survival demands that the pride uses total
teamwork to stalk, ambush and kill its prey.
Providing food for the pride can be compared
to providing income for the business.

There are four factors essential to hunting
success:

INDIVIDUALS: Each individual member
                    is powerful

GOALS: The total focus is
                    on clear-cut and
                    realistic goals

COMMUNICATION: Team members
                    must be alert to
                    communication

INCENTIVES: Motivate and
                    reward success

INDIVIDUALS

A 130 KILOGRAM LIONESS packs a lethal punch and can sprint 100 metres in six seconds. Sheathed inside each velvet paw she keeps four razored killing claws and high on the inside foreleg a hooked dew-claw to grip her prey. Equipped with strong, sharp teeth, she has sensitive ears and an acute sense of smell. As with most cats, the lioness has amazing night vision – the darker the night the more dangerous she is.

In the heat and fury of the hunt the fear-crazed zebra gallops, lashing out with his hindlegs, sometimes shattering the forelegs and jawbone of his huntress.

The fast and powerful lioness in this photograph became a specialist at ducking under the mulekick – catching the zebra high on

the shoulder and employing a mighty paw to drag down the muzzle and throw it head over heels. With the animal on the ground her team mates come charging in to help. Within seconds the pride is upon it and feasting.

Her prowess has supplied food for herself and the pride.
She feeds as an equal and demands no special morsel as a reward. Her place in the team is secure. It is simply that of an amazingly powerful specialist hunter.

There is no secret formula which makes strong teams out of weak individuals.

Powerful teams are made up of powerful individuals.

GOALS

BUFFALO ARE RIGHTLY classed among the big five and have savagely earned their reputation as one of Africa's most dangerous animals. Bad-tempered, unpredictable and built like a battleship, the buffalo bull weighs in at some 750 kilograms of well-muscled beef and bone. He is equipped with a pair of horns like the grim reaper's scythe and has a belligerent glare. The sentry bulls which stand guard over the herd are particularly dangerous.

Lion prides which hope to feast on buffalo must adopt classic techniques, such as those used by a pride of six lionesses in Botswana's Okavango Delta.

The waterways of the delta are dotted with islands of lush grazing. The small pride sat concealed on one of these and focussed on a herd of about 250 massive buffalo trawling the shallows. Before the herd arrived at the lions' island, fifteen or so of the younger bulls began grazing on a smaller mound of land – a bad mistake which left the herd only half guarded when it trudged up out of the water.

An experienced older lioness sprang up from her hiding place and charged down on the main herd. Five guard bulls were still on watch and sped after the lone lioness who led them off on a wild decoy chase through the bushes. With the cows and calves left unprotected the pride raced in for the kill. The bulls, alerted by the bellowing, came stampeding back, but, on this run, the wily old lioness ran obstruction in front of them and slowed down their return.

The pride pulled back but a plump cow had already been slaughtered.

When the mighty herd rumbled away, the lions crept out of the grass to feed on their kill.

Nothing had been allowed to distract the pride from its purpose. From the moment the buffalo were spotted, each team member was utterly focussed on the common goal, alert to the task and literally quivering with anticipation.

In the middle of a buffalo hunt a lioness will not suddenly start chasing warthogs.

The pride focusses intently on clearly understood and realistic goals.

COMMUNICATION

AS WITH MOST CATS, lions hunt best in the dark.

The pride rests in the heat of the day and stirs only in the late afternoon.

They form a semi-circle at one side of the pool and begin to drink their fill.

The still of the African dusk is now disturbed by the noisy slapping of rough tongues on the cool water – grunts and sighs of pleasure.

While the lions drink a distant impala gives a nervous cough – PAH! PAH!

Seven of the lions hear nothing above the splashing of water – only the young male, second from the right in the picture, hears the sound and immediately freezes – head up – amber eyes focussed.

Within two seconds all the heads are up and the great cats are fully alert.

Just one lion has heard the impala – just one of the pride has sensed something but in that instant all the team members have committed their unquestioning support.

The impala coughs again – PAH! PAH!

The pride at once divides into two groups – encircles the pool and heads for the sound.

Ten minutes later it is all over – the impala is dead. The lions are feeding.

Success has been achieved silently, swiftly and with no hesitation or communication blocks.

Each member of the pride is pro-active for their own and the group's survival.

There is no ego inside a lion pride and no complaints about not getting the MD's memo on the subject of impalas.

Team members must be alert to communication.

INCENTIVES

Lions HAVE A SIMPLE incentive scheme: if you kill, you eat
– if you don't, you starve. This translates into a 100% incentive scheme
in which success is rewarded with food and failure means starvation
and death.

A team may be motivated by anything – acknowledgement, respect, money; for the pride it is meat, and the simple lesson from lions is:

Incentives motivate and reward success.

RAISING THE CUBS

As WELL AS PROVIDING food, the lionesses give birth to and raise their cubs. They protect them and train them to be productive members of the pride – much as any new team member might be introduced into a company.

There are four factors essential to this process:

SPIRIT: Consists of trust, confidence, respect, and pride

STRUCTURE: The structure is flat

RECRUITMENT: Strict selection ensures there are no passengers

TRAINING: Is intense

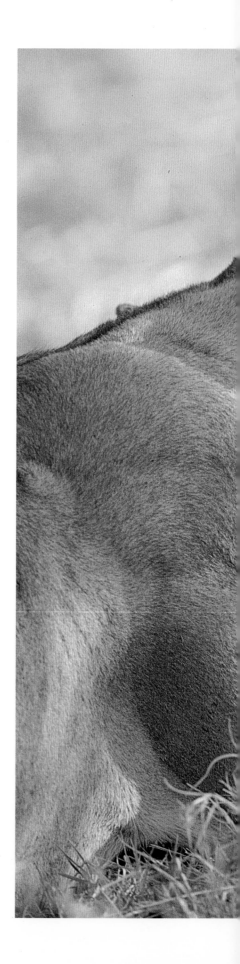

SPIRIT

WITH THE FIRST COOLING breeze of evening the pride stirs in anticipation of the night's hunting.

The great cats lick one another – rub their faces cheek-to-cheek – prowl, purr, pounce in play and softly maul their bodies together. This physical contact bonds the team as a hunting unit in an aura of confidence and pride.

Such team spirit is based on solid respect for one another's proven hunting ability and a complete trust of total support in the hunt. The trust that enables a lone lioness to cling to a zebra's shoulder after her first lunge has missed the throat – the trust repaid when her pride-mates rush to help her with the kill.

Trust, confidence, respect, and pride. The hallmarks of team spirit.

RAISING THE CUBS

An adult lion may have as many as a dozen lionesses in his pride. They usually all come into heat at the same time and insist on mating with the male to ensure his cubs are all born and raised together. This menstrual synchronisation is thought to be due to the chemistry of pheromones transferred during the lionesses' constant physical contact.

Mating with a dozen eager partners may seem like a fun way to lose weight but remember the male lion is capable of mating every 20 minutes for days on end – with each and every one of his lionesses.

At the end of the season he is just spare ribs and a broad smile!

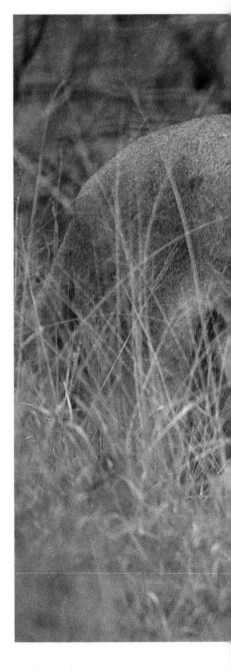

STRUCTURE

NIGHTMARES COME TRUE the day you walk into a lioness with cubs. You get only one warning – a low growl thick with menace.

It is obvious that you are living dangerously when you mess with mother love, but the lioness is especially lethal because she has invested everything in her cubs.

Mature lionesses in the pride have knowledge, weight, power and experience but these qualities need to be supplemented by the sheer speed and energy of youth if the pride is to cover all its options and be completely effective.

She has invested her future and the future of the pride in those cubs. The magic of the pride structure is that when the lioness looks after her cubs she is looking after the pride and she herself benefits from the pride's strength.

Everybody wins.

The pride operates best when it contains as many powerful hunters and fighters as possible. There are no corporate ladders to climb and no misplaced egos. A lion pride is not one of those organizations where potential talent is deliberately suppressed and the business suffers in consequence.

The structure of a lion pride is flat. It works better that way.

RAISING THE CUBS

The lionesses mate, give birth and raise their cubs as a collective group.

In this pride there are four lionesses and seventeen cubs.

Simple arithmetic says there are too many mouths to feed.
Not all the cubs will survive.
The selection begins.

RECRUITMENT

THE LIONS MUST FEED if the pride is to live. That means an animal has to die.

A warthog is by no means a big kill – scant reward for the hunt – but none of the hungry mouths scorn the smallness of the prize. Seventeen jaws tear at the flesh, eating as they have killed – with total aggression.

Even in play the cubs quickly learn to keep up with the chase and shadow their tutor's every move – to be serious about getting a full belly.

Any cub less than committed to keeping up gets left behind – performs poorly in the hunt, arrives too late to eat and goes hungry, does not gain strength, becomes listless, vulnerable, apathetic and soon enough is dead.

That was the fate of nine of the seventeen cubs whose pride brought down the warthog.

The pride can support only so many members. Places on the team can go only to the very best and have to be earned the hard way. Anything less would be treachery. Selection may mean death to an individual but it guarantees the continued life, power and excellence of the pride.

There is no such thing as a free meal.

Strict selection ensures there are no passengers.

TRAINING

LION CUBS ARE ENCOURAGED to indulge in creative play where the name of the game is – learn from your mistakes.

Opportunities come whenever times are fine.

The kill had been a wildebeest, large and succulent, and the hunters have gorged till their bloated bellies drag on the ground. Now they relax under a tree by a waterhole and tolerantly watch their ambitious cubs try to stalk a distant herd of yet more wildebeest.

The youngsters throw themselves with vigour into the pursuit of the great grey gnus who have long since seen and heard them crashing through the veld. When the cubs arrive at the killing fields the wildebeest are gone.

However, the next time the cubs accompany their mothers hunting they will have learned to notice her actions as she spots game. She freezes, one foot in the air. Only when her quarry drops its head to continue grazing does the huntress glide in, flat as a carpet, to the ambush and attack.

When the cub next plays hide-and-seek with his sister he tries to apply the lessons he has learned. Crouching low he slides in as flat as he can – freezes – measures the distance and pounces on his sister from behind a strategic bush.

The lionesses lend the tails they so lazily flick to the training schedule.

From behind a bush a tassel flashes. The cub stalks the waving tail – pounces on it from ambush and kills it. With the forgetfulness of a kitten he wanders off. Soon the tail comes back to life – temptingly waves its tassel and the game is on again.

Creative killing play is encouraged as part of a training process which is intensive and never ends.

Mistakes are to be learned from and when bellies are full the cubs are allowed to practise on big game.

Training is intense.

RAISING THE CUBS

Life for an adolescent lion cub in the security of a pride is mostly fun and games. By the time puberty approaches, in the third year of life, the young male is a powerful and handsome 130 kilograms. The hunt is going well and he is able to amble along at the rear of the action flexing his muscles and playing the fool. He is confident enough to climb in and cuff weaker animals off the kill before eating his unearned fill.

Things are about to change.

The sister who until now was his playmate comes into season and, as with junior studs everywhere, the young male's attention turns to thoughts of lust. He lets his tongue hang out.

At this point the breeding males begin to see him as a sexual rival to be swiftly gotten rid of.

When the young male climbs into the next kill he is driven off with a mighty smack on the head.

When the feasting is over and the pride rests up in the welcome shade, five hungry adolescents are left to sweat in the hot sun.

Uncomfortable, unwanted and unfed, the quintet decides to leave home and carve out a new future. They walk away from their father's domain and find themselves wandering across another's territory – but the brutes who control it are not family. They are battle-scarred veteran breeding males with everything to lose, who view the nomads as a threat to life itself. A meeting with them can end only one way.

Unaware of danger, the young lions ignore the chatter of monkeys, the warning bird-calls and the barking impala. These are, after all, familiar alarm signals which have always marked the progress of the pride.

The adult lions defending their territory – listen. For them each sound has urgent meaning and experience has taught them what to do.

From a small ridge they scout the unprotected nomads. An ambush is silently planned and swiftly executed. Within moments the trap is ready to be sprung.

Unsuspecting, the first wanderer enters a nearby reedbed. He is at once charged down by two fully grown males. Within seconds two of the young intruders are dead and the third is being torn apart. Two of them – one with a vicious gash on his hindquarters – are lucky to escape.

These survivors are chased for 10 kilometres – to the limit of the breeding males' territory.

The two nomads learn. Now, when a monkey chatters and clucks, they sit bolt upright. Alone and unprotected they sleep fitfully and when they do feed it is on scavenged scraps. Males they meet will try to kill them.

However, those who see it through become fight-hardened hunters in their own right. Powerful killers who will one day conquer an established male and earn the right to take over his space – his lionesses.

This nomadic male is about seven years old. He has been alone since his brothers were killed. He is an incredibly potent hunter who has just brought down a ton of giraffe.

Soon – in six months or a year – he will challenge a pride male.

SECURITY

SUCCESSFUL MALE LIONS have to secure sufficient territory for their lionesses to hunt and raise their cubs in a peaceful environment.

It is the responsibility of the male lion to protect his territory from competitors. Chief among these are other prides and nomadic males.

Nomads who have no territory of their own will try to take over an existing pride. When this happens the adult male is chased away or killed. Since the lioness can rear only one litter at a time the intruder will often kill her cubs, mate with her and so stamp his authority on the pride.

Businessmen might recognise this as a hostile take-over bid or as keeping a competitor out of your market.

Security depends on two main elements:

IMAGE: Enhances function

SYNERGY: The pride is more powerful than the sum of the strengths of its individuals

SECURITY

IMAGE

IN A WORLD WHERE THE choice is fight or flight, the male lion's appearance is perfectly suited to his function in the pride.

His looks alone would scare away any but the bravest competitor. He is not looking for an unnecessary fight and would prefer to frighten off the opposition.

His image tells the world he is in peak fighting condition

– a superbly trained and fully alert killing machine. He weighs in at 230 kilograms, has five knives in each fist and a roar that makes the earth quake.

That magnificent mane is not just there to keep out the cold – it is a part of his high-profile image, a clear signal to any marauder. He is tough enough to defend his territory – sexy enough to entice his harem.

SECURITY

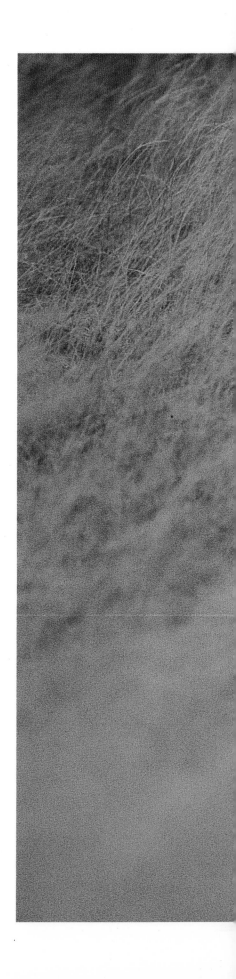

In a lion pride where the image of each member is directly related to their function in the team, the lioness employs a low profile – sleek, smooth, low to the ground and lethally swift she subtly blends into the background.

Her image perfectly suits her purpose in the pride.

She is sudden death unseen, waiting in hidden ambush.

Image enhances function.

SYNERGY

HERE IS A PHOTOGRAPH of the two surviving brothers from the party of five that were booted out of the pride.

One of the brothers boldly faces the light. From his attitude and from the look on that face you can see he has changed. He has been a nomad for three long, hard years – lost three brothers and all of his sense of humour.

This is not the same cub who looked on life as mostly fun and games, but an adult male approaching his prime.

He wants territory. He wants lionesses. He knows he will have to fight but he is tired of running. He is ready. He has even selected his target.

Cool, dark night descends on the veld and the big black-maned breeding male stretches and roars.

The two nomads rise silently and begin to stalk him. They ignore kudu and zebra in their path. Both are committed to an identical goal and are totally focussed on it.

Monkeys chatter the alarm.

Big Black turns his head to listen and he and the nomads stare into each other's eyes at 100 metres.

Big Black displays his most fearsome image for them – warning them off.

The pair have seen it all before and the bolder of the two immediately smashes head-on into Big Black, huge paws dealing out mighty blows. His brother runs behind Big Black and attempts to bite through his backbone to paralyse him for the kill.

Big Black is fighting for his life on two fronts – all three lions twisting and turning in clouds of dust. Bushes are crushed. Roaring, snarling, biting, hitting out with paws and claws they tumble into a donga, burst apart and Big Black comes out running.

SECURITY

The brothers, sensing victory, chase him.

This way and that way he cuts, backwards and forwards across his territory but the chase continues.

In the heat of the day the pursuers rest.

And for four nights the chase continues.

Morning of the fifth day is damp and overcast when Big Black finds his pride of lionesses. They are hunting kudu along a dry river bed. A kudu bull is cut out of the herd and killed in a left and right ambush set by two lionesses operating a pincer movement with military precision.

Big Black has been on the run. He is hungry.

Cuffing cubs and lionesses alike he clears them off the kill and begins to gorge himself.

In one sitting he fills his belly with more than 30 kilograms of fresh meat and then sleeps all day under a tree.

It would seem to go against the ethic of the pride to allow a lion his fill when it has not been earned. Big Black took no part in the hunt – he is a breeding male in serious danger of losing his territory, his lionesses and his life.

It would seem his presence as a passenger is a disadvantage to the pride – but the last act of the drama has not yet been played out.

That night the nomads catch up and the chase is on again.

And so it continues – night after night for another four nights.

On the morning of the ninth day the lionesses kill a zebra foal and once again Big Black is first to the feast. This time he devours the entire zebra by himself and once more sleeps all day in the cool shade.

SECURITY

This picture of Big Black was taken on his eleventh day of being hunted.

His image is intact – in fact he is in magnificent condition and ready for anything.

For ten nights in a row he has been a fugitive but, throughout the life and death run, he has been experienced enough to duck and dive within his own domain.

He has maintained contact with his hunting team and they have provided him with a zebra and a kudu. His image says he has eaten, he has rested and his pride is still in place.

By stark contrast the nomads are starting to look bedraggled. They have no territory – no team in place to feed them.

After eleven days of charging aggression it is becoming difficult for them to remain motivated – harder for them to run shoulder to shoulder.

The weaker of the two loses interest in the pursuit and falls far behind.

Big Black seizes this moment to divide and rule. He makes a series of mock charges towards the remaining intruder – allowing the nomad almost to make contact before turning and fleeing once more.

Six times this happens and each time he draws the bolder brother away from his partner – splitting up the team.

At the seventh mock charge he stops as before, growls, turns tail when charged and runs down a steep donga to crouch behind long grass at the bottom.

His attacker, following at full speed, skids down the steep slope and stops in the sand searching for Big Black.

SECURITY

Crash-tackle! There is no warning bell, just a blinding bolt of lethal aggression as Big Black surges up out of hiding and stuns his opponent with a brutal blow on the side of the head. Then both massive paws hook into the head and pull it towards waiting teeth. Big Black crunches down hard on the nomad's skull – his fangs sink deep. The lone nomad is seconds from death.

It is only now, at this extreme moment, that the second brother arrives to back up his partner.

Big Black unclenches his jaws and turns to face the new threat. The injured lion stumbles free and scrabbles up the slope through a vision blurred by blood, matted hair and agony. It will take him nine cruel months to recover from his wounds and be ready again to enter the arena. His partner, seeing his brother's head almost destroyed, turns tail and flees with him.

Big Black roared his victory as the nomads fled. Later he headed for the dry river bed where his lionesses were lying in the cool sand. He was a brave fighter and a brilliant tactician, but without his pride behind him, he would have been dead.

SECURITY

The nomads retreat, as distant from Big Black as possible. Nine cruel months cringing in the bush recovering from a nearly fatal brawl has taught the nomads the value of teamwork. That which has not killed them has made them strong. They have learned the lessons of survival and now behave as though they are joined at the hip. Two powerful individuals operating as one single entity. This attitude brings success and is rewarded with food and the gaining of strength and confidence.

Now they decide to attack a different territory, a different pride male.

This time, they are ready.

This time, the attack is hard, fast and totally aggressive.

A lioness is the first to die. Then her three cubs. Some pride members, attempting to fight, are savagely slashed.

Swiftly, silently, the hunting team is destroyed – unable to hunt.

The two nomads slide away and watch. And wait.

They locate the pride male and strike again. A relentless running battle ensues.

The male survives their savage attack but his eye is gouged out in the fight, one back leg is severely gashed and he limps badly from a torn shoulder.

Weakening rapidly, he barely manages to avoid his pursuers.

Two days later the nomads catch him and kill him.

Within hours of his death his cubs have been slaughtered. His lionesses newly mated.

In fight after fight it is the pride which holds together as a team that wins – the pride which uses all the skills and resources of all its members that is victorious.

The pride is more powerful than the sum of the strengths of its individuals.

CONCLUSION

LESSONS FROM LIONS

IT MAY SEEM A HARSH universal law which dictates that only the successful survive, but is it any different in the business jungle?

The pride has evolved as a potent example of teamwork for maximum effect. Their combined co-operative effort working towards a common objective leads to a winning team situation where both the pride and the individual thrive.

The lesson from lions to business is – teams are successful because:
* Each individual member is powerful
* The total focus is on clear-cut and realistic goals
* Team members are alert to communication
* Incentives motivate and reward success
* Spirit consists of trust, confidence, respect, and pride
* The structure is flat
* Strict selection ensures there are no passengers
* Training is intense
* Image enhances function
* Synergy – the pride is more powerful than the sum of the strengths of its individuals.

The unremitting application of these ten power points puts the pride in a win-win situation: *the pride and its members thrive.*

The business and the individuals thrive.

THE END